Amenhotep III was probably the vainest pharaoh. He had himself portrayed more than any other king and well over 1,000 representations of him have survived.

Four million embalmed **ibises** were discovered at a single animal cemetery at Saqqara, each in its own individual pot.

BY JAMES PUTNAM & JEREMY PEMBERTON

AMAZING
FACTS
ABOUT ANCIENT
EGYPT

THAMES AND HUDSON

CONTENTS

Introduction **5**

King Tut **6**

Other Famous Kings **12**

Famous Queens **18**

Pyramids & Other Wonders **22**

Food & Drink **28**

Health, Beauty & Love **32**

Work & Play **38**

War, Crime & Punishment **44**

Science & Ancient Wisdom **48**

Magic, Myth & Mystery **52**

Mummies & Tomb-Robbers **58**

Beginner's Guide **64**

INTRODUCTION

The ancient Egyptians created a civilization that lasted for over 3,000 years. It has been calculated that during this period more than half a billion people existed on Egypt's soil.

The Egyptians developed a remarkable knowledge of astronomy, engineering, mathematics and medicine, and had an organized taxation and legal system with a police force and courts.

Women had more legal rights than those in some countries today. They wore fine clothing, and used a wide range of cosmetics and beauty products.

Tutankhamun and Ramesses the Great were just two of the 170 or more known pharaohs of Egypt. Pepi II was the longest reigning king in recorded history. He ruled for 94 years and lived to the age of 97.

We owe our calendar of 365 days to the ancient Egyptians. They were the first to divide the day and night into 24 hours and to use clocks.

The ancient Egyptians were truly amazing.

Tutankhamun was neither an important pharaoh, nor a successful one. But he is the most famous pharaoh, thanks to the discovery of his incredible tomb by Howard Carter and Lord Carnarvon in 1922.

When Tut became king, the Great Pyramid had already been standing for some 1,250 years.

When he died, aged only 18, his tomb was robbed twice soon after the burial.

According to Howard Carter, the ancient **robbers** got away with about 60 per cent of the jewellery originally deposited in the tomb.

Carter spent about 5 years looking for Tut's tomb, 8 years clearing it and almost 10 years cataloguing the 5,000 objects found in it. He never published a full account of his amazing discoveries.

On the day the tomb was opened, Carter's pet **canary** was swallowed by a cobra.

The clearance of the **antechamber** took 7 weeks and used up more than a mile of cotton wadding and 32 bales of calico.

Sometime after the discovery of the tomb, the **phallus** went missing from the mummy of the king.

Tut's **tomb** was originally intended for someone else. The sarcophagus and other artifacts had been made for one of his predecessors.

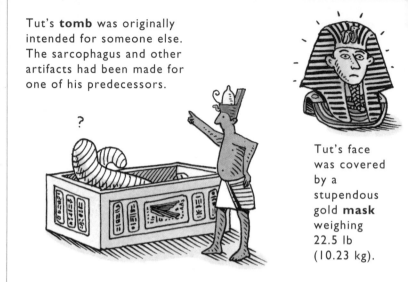

Tut's face was covered by a stupendous gold **mask** weighing 22.5 lb (10.23 kg).

Tut's body lay within 3 **mummy cases** or coffins, which fit inside one another like Russian dolls. The innermost coffin is made of 22 carat gold and weighs 296 lb (110.9 kg).

The **scrap value** alone of the innermost coffin is reckoned at £1 million or $1.5 million.

The largest of the 3 **shrines** around the sarcophagus is big enough to hold a medium-sized car.

A personal **first-aid kit** was found in Tut's tomb, which included bandages and a finger-sling.

Carter estimated there to have been 350 litres of **precious oils** stored mostly in stone vessels. Two vessels still bore the fingermarks of the ancient tomb-robbers.

Tut was not alone in his tomb. The mummified bodies of his 2 still-born **daughters** were found in tiny coffins in the so-called Treasury.

King Tut was probably a dedicated **follower of fashion**. He would have used the wooden dummy or mannequin found in the tomb to model his vast array of clothes.

Tut's 'christening' **shawl** is made of the finest linen ever discovered. Textile experts estimate that it took 9 months of 11-hour days to make.

Over 150 amulets and other items of **jewellery** had been placed on and around the King's body.

The King had almost 100 items of **footwear**, made from leather, basketwork, wood and even sheet-gold.

Tutankhamun's '**wine list**' contained a choice of some thirty varieties: many jars had labels noting the wine, year, vineyard, and vintner.

More than a hundred **loin-cloths** and about 30 gloves or chariot gauntlets were found in the tomb.

Thirty **boomerangs** were found in Tutankhamun's tomb, designed to stun and return when hunting animals.

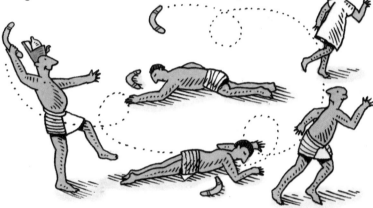

The world's first '**sofa-bed**' is the folding campaign bed of Tutankhamun with its sophisticated hinging.

In 1939, Tutankhamun's **trumpet** was blown for the first time in 3,000 years. The sound was broadcast on the radio and recorded for posterity.

If Tutankhamun is the most famous pharaoh, his father Akhenaten must be the most controversial. In appearance he looked almost like a woman, and he scandalized Egypt by overturning the established religion to worship a single god.

Akhenaten's own father, Amenhotep III, was more of a typical, boastful pharaoh. He claimed to have killed 56 wild bulls in a single hunt.

Ramesses the Great, however, was Egypt's mightiest pharaoh. A prodigious builder and proud warrior, he sired over 100 children during his 66-year reign.

Ramesses the Great had 8 official wives and nearly 100 concubines. He was over 90 years old when he died in 1212 BC.

Ramesses outlived 12 of his sons. When the 13th son, Merneptah, finally succeeded to the throne, he was already an old man.

In 1881 **Ramesses**' mummy was discovered in a cache of 40 mummies at Deir el Bahri. Nearly a hundred years later, the mummy was flown to Paris for treatment under a passport listing its occupation as 'king (deceased)'.

X-rays of **Ramesses**' mummy revealed that his nose was packed with peppercorns to preserve its characteristic hooked shape. The king suffered badly from arthritis of the hip, heart disease and abscesses in his jaw.

Atchoo!

Apart from Ramesses the Great (Ramesses II), 10 other pharaohs bore the name **Ramesses** in the 13th–12th centuries BC.

Ramesses III had boats hauled overland to the Red Sea and sent them sailing down to Punt (Somalia) to acquire myrrh for incense.

Tuthmosis III, who lived in the 15th century BC, was probably the first pharaoh to have pierced ears. He was a great hunter and claimed to have killed 120 elephants, as well as 120 wild bulls in just an hour and 7 lions 'in the blink of an eye'.

Tuthmosis tried to destroy the memory of his predecessor, Queen Hatshepsut, by building a wall around one of her obelisks. Ironically, this helped preserve it for posterity.

Amenhotep II was renowned for his physical strength. None of his soldiers could draw his bow. On one occasion he drew 300 bows and fired the arrows straight through targets of copper.

Amenhotep III was probably the vainest pharaoh. He had himself portrayed more than any other king and well over 1,000 representations of him have survived.

Amenhotep III's most famous statues, the so-called Colossi of Memnon at Thebes, originally stood 70 ft (21 m) high. Each is carved from a single block of quartzite transported from quarries over 400 miles away. In ancient times a crack in one of the statues caused it to emit an eerie wail at dawn and dusk, which astonished several Roman emperors who visited Thebes.

WOOOH.....

Amenhotep III dug a pleasure lake for his wife, which was over 5,500 ft (1,700 m) long, in only 15 days. One of Amenhotep's brides, a princess from the kingdom of Mitanni (northern Iraq), arrived in Egypt with 317 servantwomen.

Akhenaten's devotion to a single god has led people to call him a forerunner of Moses and of Christ.

Akhenaten's strange physique led one Egyptologist in the 19th century to claim he was a woman masquerading as a man.

All **Akhenaten**'s temples and monuments were torn down after his death and his name expunged from inscriptions and other records.

The Nubian pharaoh **Taharqa** had his soldiers undertake a cross-country run of 30 miles across the desert in four hours, accompanying them in his chariot.

Four queens ruled Egypt in their own right. Two are obscure: Sobekneferu and Twosret. Two are famous: Hatshepsut and Cleopatra. But many other queens wielded immense influence, and one – the beautiful Nefertiti, wife of Akhenaten – may have held sole power after her husband's death.

In 1925 the tomb of **Queen Hetepheres**, mother of King Khufu, was found accidentally near the Giza pyramids when a photographer's tripod leg sank into a hidden shaft. It is the only intact royal burial from the Old Kingdom ever discovered, revealing some of the finest examples of ancient Egyptian furniture and jewellery.

Queen Hatshepsut is probably the first known horticulturalist and zoologist. In 1490 BC she sent a special expedition to the Land of Punt (in Somalia) to bring back myrrh trees to plant in Egypt as well as exotic animals for a zoo, including giraffes and rhinoceroses.

Hatshepsut was referred to as 'His Majesty', despite being a woman. After her succession she was depicted as a man, without breasts and wearing the costume of a ruling pharaoh, complete with false beard.

Hatshepsut reigned as regent for her nephew and stepson Tuthmosis III. When the queen died, Tuthmosis erased her name from monuments and broke all her statues.

The tomb of **Queen Nefertari** – wife of Ramesses the Great – is the most beautifully painted of all the royal tombs and has been nicknamed 'Egypt's Sistine Chapel'.

Seven Egyptian queens bore the name **Cleopatra**. Only the final, famous one ruled Egypt in her own right.

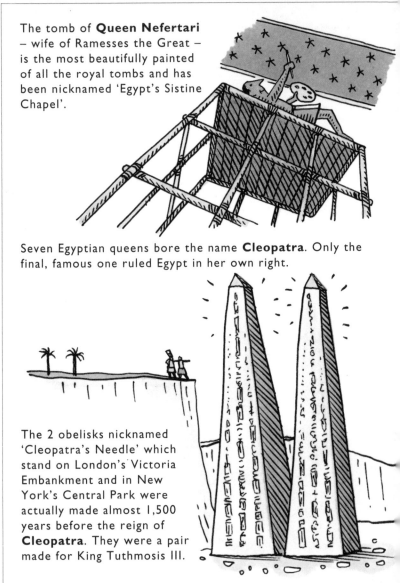

The 2 obelisks nicknamed 'Cleopatra's Needle' which stand on London's Victoria Embankment and in New York's Central Park were actually made almost 1,500 years before the reign of **Cleopatra**. They were a pair made for King Tuthmosis III.

The earliest film about **Cleopatra** was made in France in 1899. The 1963 epic, *Cleopatra*, besides being the most expensive film ever made up to that time, was also one of the biggest box office flops. In one scene Cleopatra, played by Elizabeth Taylor, enters Rome on a sphinx almost the same size as the Great Sphinx of Giza. The movie also featured a barge belching out pink smoke.

Cleopatra seduced Julius Caesar and bore him a son. Later the 'temptress of the East' married Mark Antony, by whom she had three more children.

After their defeat at the battle of Actium, Mark Antony and **Cleopatra** committed suicide – she, according to legend, from the bite of an asp.

Of the Seven Wonders of the Ancient World, only the pyramids at Giza remain standing. There are at least 80 pyramids in Egypt, and another 130 smaller ones built later in the Sudan.

Pyramids were the tombs of pharaohs, but no royal mummies have ever been found inside them. Ancient tomb-robbers got there first.

The **pyramids** were built not by slaves, but largely by peasant farmers conscripted during their 'off-season', when their fields were flooded by the annual inundation of the Nile.

The first **pyramids** were actually mounds that proceeded in a series of steps towards the top – hence the name, 'step pyramid'.

The true **pyramid** shape may have been inspired by the spreading rays of the sun.

The **Step Pyramid** at Saqqara, 200 ft (60 m) high, is the oldest monumental building in the world, and the earliest surviving pyramid. Built around 2650 BC for King Djoser, it has a maze of underground passages – more than any other pyramid.

King Snefru had not 1 but 3 **pyramids** – no one knows why.

At Meidum, the Egyptians hit on the idea of 'filling in the steps' of what had been a step pyramid, to convert it into the first **true pyramid**. Unfortunately the structure collapsed.

23

Napoleon estimated that the blocks of stone from the 3 **Giza pyramids** would have been sufficient to build a wall 10 ft (3 m) high around the whole of France.

The white limestone blocks that once covered the **Giza pyramids** would have looked blindingly bright in the midday sun. Much of this fine stone was plundered in later times to build monuments such as the Mosque of Mohammed Ali.

The **Great Pyramid** of King Khufu took 23 years to build. During that time, on average one block of stone would have been put in position every 5 minutes.

There are about 2.3 million blocks of stone in the **Great Pyramid** at Giza, some weighing a colossal 15 tons, or more than 2 African bull elephants.

At 481 ft (146 m), the **Great Pyramid** was the tallest building on earth until the Eiffel Tower was erected in 1889.

The area covered by the **Great Pyramid** is vast enough to hold the cathedrals of Florence, Milan and St. Peter's in Rome, as well as St. Paul's and Westminster Abbey in London.

The outer casing blocks of the **Great Pyramid** were so skilfully cut that it is impossible to run a knife between them.

The **Great Sphinx** at Giza is the largest freestanding sculpture that survives from the ancient world. Over 240 ft (73 m) long, and 66 ft (20 m) high, it is probably a colossal portrait of King Khafre, whose huge pyramid rises behind it.

An Emir in the Middle Ages wiped the smile from the face of the **Great Sphinx** by firing at it with cannons.

Tuthmosis IV, while still a young prince, rested one day beside the **Great Sphinx** and had a dream. The sun god promised to make him pharaoh if he freed the sphinx from the sand. Tuthmosis cleared the sand and duly became king.

The largest known **statue** in the world ever to have been cut from a single block of granite (one of the hardest stones) stood in the funerary temple of Ramesses the Great at Thebes. Fragments of an even larger statue have been found at Tanis where the size of the big toe equals that of a man's body.

The orientation of Ramesses the Great's huge **temple at Abu Simbel** was amazingly precise. At spring and autumn equinox the sun shone directly into the giant chamber, illuminating the statue of the king inside.

Long before the Suez Canal, a **waterway** was built c. 600 BC to link the Mediterranean with the Red Sea. It can still be traced running parallel to the modern canal for part of its course.

FOOD & DRINK

The Egyptians had a mostly vegetarian, and quite healthy, diet – although the grit in their bread flour tended to grind down their teeth.

They also enjoyed fish and fowl. Roast goose was the favourite dish for special occasions and religious festivals. Beer was the most popular beverage, and drunkenness was quite common.

Over 50 varieties of **bread** are known for the New Kingdom, some baked in the shape of animals.

Fish were sacred in the city of Oxyrhynchus. A war is reputed to have broken out between this city and a neighbouring town whose inhabitants enjoyed eating fish.

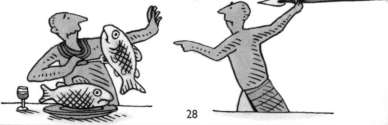

The Egyptians were one of the first peoples to hatch **eggs** artificially. This was achieved by burying them in dung hills which produced the required heat.

The working man's **packed lunch** usually consisted of bread, beer and onions, with an occasional cucumber.

Besides being written on, the young shoots of the **papyrus** plant were also eaten like bamboo shoots.

Baboons were trained to climb fig trees and pick the ripe fruit for their owners.

The wealthy frequently liked to be depicted with rolls of **fat** around their midriffs to suggest prosperity and success.

In paintings of banquets a **mandrake** fruit is sometimes shown being held to the noses of guests for its hallucinatory properties.

Early texts warn students to stay away from **beer halls** and women of ill repute.

Egyptian **beer** was thick and lumpy, and had to be filtered through a strainer.

At the annual festival of Hathor, vast quantities of beer were handed out to the pilgrims. It was believed that **intoxication** could lead to religious ecstasy.

A famous Theban tomb painting shows men being carried from a **drinking party**; another shows a woman throwing-up after drinking too much wine.

It is recorded that the pharaoh Amosis abandoned affairs of state for a **drinking bout**.

Beer-making was done by women as well as men. There were over 17 varieties, as well as more expensive 'import' beers from Syria and Nubia.

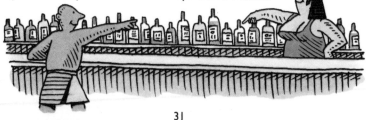

In the ancient world, Egyptian doctors were renowned for their skill and expertise. Greek medicine was greatly influenced by them, and their remedies form the basis of much of modern herbal medicine.

Egyptian perfumes and essential oils were likewise famous in ancient times. Beauty aids flourished in the New Kingdom, when love poems too became fashionable.

The human **body** was divided up into 36 parts and each part came under the protection of a god or goddess.

When a remedy was prescribed by a doctor, it sometimes came in a container with a **prescription** written on it, like our labelled bottles nowadays.

Circumcision was practised for pharaohs, priests and officials.

Priests were required to **bathe** twice a day and twice during the night.

Aphrodisiacs made from the cos lettuce and the mandrake root were used.

Medical texts contain prescriptions for **female contraceptives** such as crocodile dung and honey. Another potion included frankincense, celery and cow's milk.

The earliest **toilet seat** in the world comes from the city of Akhetaten, c. 1350 BC. Here toilets with wood, pottery and stone seats were placed above large bowls of sand.

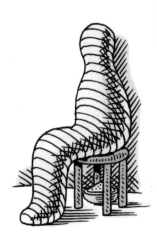

Some of the early royal tombs from c. 2750 BC even included **lavatories**.

The Egyptians were among the first to attempt **dentistry**. Some mummies have teeth filled with a kind of mineral cement made from resin and malachite. In other mummies, gold wire has been used to bind loose teeth like a 'dental bridge'.

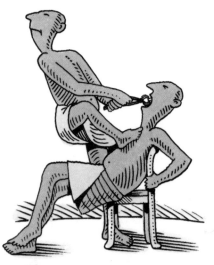

Dancing girls and children frequently shaved their heads. Some women had **tattoos**.

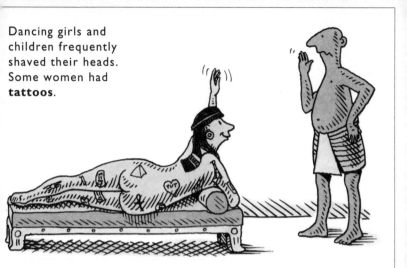

Ritual **false beards** were worn by kings to denote royalty and even Queen Hatshepsut had one.

Kohl **eyeliner** used by millions of women today was invented by the Egyptians, and helped protect the eyes against infection.

Incense cones of perfumed grease worn on the head were designed to melt through the course of an evening, cooling the face and giving off a pleasant aroma.

An **erotic papyrus** in the Turin Museum features 12 comic strip type stories showing the adventures of a middle-aged man (possibly a priest) and a young girl, complete with titillating captions of their conversation.

In one scene, Ramesses III is shown **nude** playing draughts or checkers with a group of scantily clad girls.

In the New Kingdom, **love songs** were recited at banquets to the accompaniment of flutes and harps: 'Your skin is like the mandragora berry'; 'Your love is in my flesh like the reed in the arms of the wind'.

Young Egyptian men preferred to wear short **kilts**, whereas their elders chose more dignified, longer ones.

Affection was expressed by rubbing noses, but mouth to mouth **kissing** was also practised.

The Egyptians had a 10-day week, and worked on 9 of them. Artisans laboured for 4 hours in the morning, broke off for a meal and a nap, and then resumed for another 4 hours in the afternoon. Absenteeism was common.

Egyptian leisure activities included wrestling, fishing, athletics, acrobatics, fencing, archery, board games, ball games, bull-fighting – and playing with pets.

One of the least desirable trades was that of **laundryman**. Not only was it ritually unclean, but there was the ever-present danger that a crocodile might snap up the hapless worker as he washed clothes in the Nile.

The Egyptians had no **money** or coinage until Persian times. Wages were paid in goods such as linen and even beans and onions.

A delay in receiving wages led to the world's earliest recorded **strike** – by workmen constructing the tomb of Ramesses III in 1150 BC.

A letter written by the Mayor of Thebes to a farmer 3,500 years ago ordered him to gather produce and chastised him for being **lazy**. One of the farmer's many sins was that he liked eating in bed.

The world's oldest sports **facility** was built around the Step Pyramid at Saqqara (c. 2600 BC). On the 30th anniversary of his coronation the pharaoh displayed his physical strength by a long-distance solo run on a special track – not unlike the jogging mania of recent US presidents.

The first recorded international **sports event** was a wrestling and quarter-staff contest between Egyptian and foreign soldiers held before Ramesses III in 1160 BC.

The oldest depiction of a **ball game** shows King Tuthmosis III with a bat and ball in 1450 BC.

The Egyptians loved **board games**, especially Senet, rather like draughts or checkers – no fewer than three sets of this game were found in Tutankhamun's tomb.

It took a **scribe** 12 years to learn to write the many hundreds of hieroglyphs in the Egyptian script. Study started at the early age of 4. Idle pupils were soundly thrashed.

Dancing girls wore belts round their hips made of special beads that jingled as they moved.

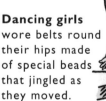

The Egyptians were probably the first people to regard **fishing** as a sport as well as a source of food. A drawing has survived which depicts a nobleman fishing with a rod and line.

The Egyptians kept all manner of **pets**, from dogs – the most popular – to monkeys, baboons, cats and geese. Many tomb paintings show the family pet lurking under the chair of the deceased, often mischievously eating food stolen from the offering table.

They were so distressed when a pet **cat** died that they shaved their eyebrows.

The Greek historian Herodotus was amazed by the Egyptian obsession with **cats**. He noted that when a house caught fire, citizens were more concerned to save their cats than to put the fire out.

The pet **dogs** of a Middle Kingdom prince are shown on his tomb wall. One, a saluki, is still known today as the 'hound of the pharaohs'.

Representations of **dogs** are often accompanied by their names – like 'Ebony', 'Black' or 'Big'.

It is recorded that in 10 BC at Lake Moeris, Egyptian priests had a pet **crocodile** which they tamed and fed with cakes and honey wine.

The Egyptians often named their children after **animals**. Among the many examples are Frog, Mouse, Gazelle, Monkey, Wolf, Hound, Crocodile and Hippopotamus.

The Egyptians were not naturally the most warlike of ancient peoples and foreign mercenaries were often employed to prop up the army. But that did not prevent New Kingdom pharaohs from glorying in their role as warrior-heroes. They frequently had themselves depicted smiting the enemy from their chariots.

The first recorded **battle** in history took place at Megiddo in Palestine in 1458 BC, when Tuthmosis III's army routed defending forces. His troops, however, were so keen to pillage the enemy camp that they neglected to capture the city, which fell only after a gruelling 7-month siege.

Chariots were only introduced halfway through Egyptian history, after 1600 BC. Before that, the army was made up entirely of **foot soldiers**.

The sons of pharaohs were sometimes made **army commanders** while they were still only infants.

At a famous battle against the Libyans, Ramesses III claimed personally to have **killed 12,535** of the enemy and to have taken over 1,000 prisoners.

Medals for courage were awarded by the pharaoh in the form of a 'fly' made out of gold (perhaps symbolic of the fly's natural persistence).

In the 15th century BC General Djehuty captured the port of Joppa (modern Jaffa) by **smuggling** 200 soldiers into the city hidden in baskets.

A New Kingdom satirist painted this gloomy picture of a **soldier's life**: 'His bread and water are carried on his back like the load of an ass. His drink is foul water. If he returns to Egypt he is like worm-eaten wood. He is brought back upon an ass: his kit has been stolen and his servant has run off.'

After a battle the Egyptians cut off the hands, tongues or phalluses of their slain opponents and stacked them in heaps so that scribes could accurately count the number of **enemy dead**.

A prince of Kadesh tried to defeat his opponents by sending a **mare** into the midst of the stallions of the Egyptian chariotry. The mare was killed, however, before she could rouse the stallions to passionate confusion.

For **treachery**, the punishment was loss of the tongue, for forgery the right hand was cut off. Noblemen and high officials found guilty of treason were honour-bound to commit suicide.

Egyptian police used **sniffer dogs** to track down criminals, just like modern police.

The ancient Greeks referred to Egypt as the cradle of science. Pythagoras is reputed to have spent many years studying their wisdom. But the Egyptians were not infallible. Their solar year of 365 days fell short of the true year by 1 day in every 4 years. As a result, even halfway through pharaonic times farmers were complaining bitterly that 'winter is come in summer, and the months come about turned backwards'.

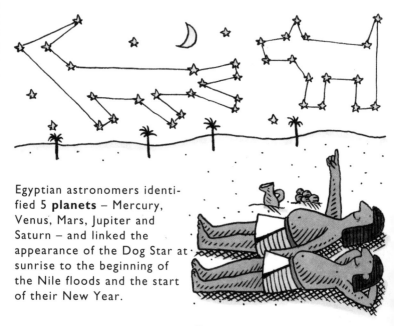

Egyptian astronomers identified **5 planets** – Mercury, Venus, Mars, Jupiter and Saturn – and linked the appearance of the Dog Star at sunrise to the beginning of the Nile floods and the start of their New Year.

The earliest report of a **shooting star,** possibly Halley's Comet, comes from the reign of Tuthmosis III c. 1450 BC.

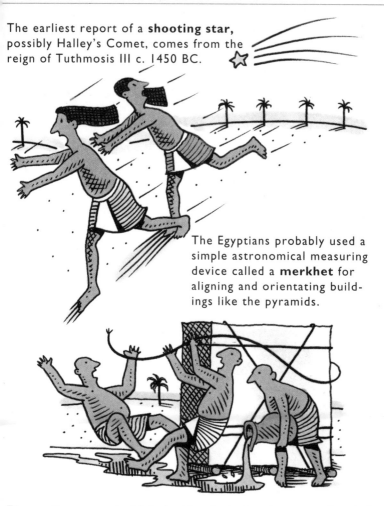

The Egyptians probably used a simple astronomical measuring device called a **merkhet** for aligning and orientating buildings like the pyramids.

The earliest record of **lubrication** is depicted on a tomb relief of c. 1850 BC where a man is shown pouring liquid to oil the road. It took about 170 sturdy men to move a 60-ton colossal statue, using sledges, levers and ropes.

The earliest mechanical device for raising water and irrigating fields was invented during the New Kingdom. Known today as the **shaduf**, this instrument uses a weighted pole balanced on a frame and is still widely employed along the Nile.

A mechanical fowling technique was developed in the Middle Kingdom that used **trigger-operated nets**.

A papyrus by the scribe Amenemope attempted to collect together all contemporary knowledge and is therefore probably the earliest surviving **encyclopedia**, dating from c. 1000 BC.

The earliest known **coin-operated machine** for dispensing water is recorded as existing at Alexandria in about 300 BC.

The oldest surviving '**book**' in the world is the so-called Prisse Papyrus, now in the Bibliothèque Nationale in Paris, dating from 2000 BC.

The longest papyrus **document** known is called the 'Great Harris' and extends for 135 ft (41 m); the widest papyrus measures 20 inches (51 cm). Both are in the British Museum.

Over 700,000 **books** were burnt when the library at Alexandria – the greatest in the ancient world – caught fire in 47 BC.

The Egyptians believed in the power of magic. If you fell ill, you needed not just a doctor but a magician to recite beneficial spells. Coffins, tomb walls and even statues were covered with magical texts to ward off evil spirits. Amulets worn on the body gave active protection.

Amun-Re and Osiris were the most famous of their gods, but they worshipped a bewildering variety of other deities and creatures as well, from the sacred bull, Apis, to the humble mongoose known as 'Pharaoh's rat'.

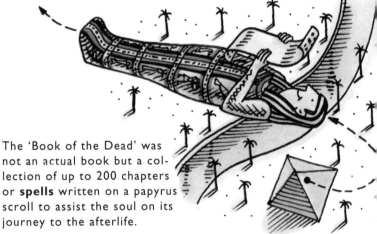

The 'Book of the Dead' was not an actual book but a collection of up to 200 chapters or **spells** written on a papyrus scroll to assist the soul on its journey to the afterlife.

A popular scene from the Book of the Dead was the so-called **Opening of the Mouth** ceremony. A statue or mummy could be brought magically back to life if the foreleg of a bull was extended towards it, and the face was touched with a fish-tail knife blade and other objects.

Fire-spitting **serpent demons** were among the most terrifying creatures in the Book of the Dead. Some had wings, others had legs. But the snake also symbolized survival because it could shed its skin.

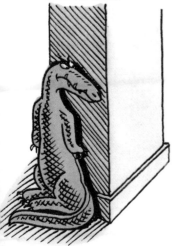

The **crocodile monster** was another nightmarish apparition in the Book of the Dead. Called the 'devourer of human hearts', it lay in wait for the deceased in the Hall of Judgment.

In predynastic times it was customary to **sacrifice** servants and slave women at the king's funeral, so that they could help their lord in the next life.

In the **Pyramid Texts**, hieroglyphs of dangerous animals such as scorpions were shown pierced with knives or with their legs cut off, to render them harmless.

The colour **red** had bad associations. On papyri, the scribes used red ink to describe evil gods and demons, but wrote in black for the rest of the text.

In dynastic times small models of workers, not sacrificed slaves, were placed in tombs to provide **magical power** for their masters. Each tomb might have 365 workers — one for each day of the year. King Seti I had over 700 in his tomb.

Black magic was used with wax figures and charms in a failed plot to kill Ramesses III. The conspirators were executed or forced to commit suicide, and 3 of the judges brought to try them had their noses and ears amputated for colluding with the rebels.

According to Egyptian beliefs, 77 **asses** stood in the way of the sun in order to try to prevent the sunrise. The hieroglyph for 'ass' bore two knives stuck between the shoulder blades to render the animal harmless.

The sun-god **Re** once wept and his tears fell to earth, turning themselves into bees.

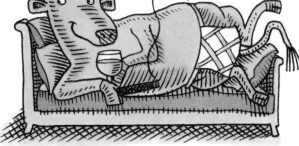

The **willow** was sacred to Osiris, god of the dead, because it had sheltered his coffin while his soul alighted upon the tree as a phoenix.

The death of the sacred **Apis bull** was a very important event. Records exist of the death, entombment and selection of each new Apis for a period of over 1,000 years. Only one bull was chosen to be Apis at any one time. It had special accommodation in the temple and was provided with a 'harem' of cows.

One of the oddest deities was **Taweret**, a hippopotamus goddess standing on her hind legs with a crocodile's tail along her back. She protected women during childbirth.

The **ibis** was the sacred animal of the god of writing, Thoth. Ibises were specially bred on a lake near Saqqara to be embalmed and sold to pilgrims for them to bury at the site.

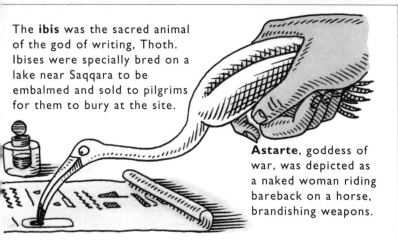

Astarte, goddess of war, was depicted as a naked woman riding bareback on a horse, brandishing weapons.

The dwarf-god **Bes** played musical instruments to frighten away evil spirits. As a protective deity his image was carved on head-rests, beds, mirrors and jars of cosmetics. He could throttle two serpents with his bare hands.

People sometimes gave **offerings** of ears carved on stones to persuade the gods to listen to their prayers.

In later Egyptian history, it became customary to spend a night in a temple, in order to receive a prophetic **dream**.

For centuries, mummies have proved a source of fascination and of wealth. During the Renaissance, ground-up mummy became a popular potion, believed to have magical healing powers. Tomb-robbers in the last century lived by selling jewellery stolen from mummy wrappings. Today the mummy has become a movie star, disturbed from eternal slumber and prowling the earth to wreak vengeance on its tormentors.

'**Mummy**' comes from the Arabic *mummiya*, meaning 'bitumen', which people in early medieval times mistakenly thought was the dark substance coating many mummies.

In order to embalm or **mummify** someone, the ancient Egyptians removed all the internal organs except the heart. In the next life, the heart would be weighed on the scales of truth. Special heart-shaped amulets were included in mummy wrappings to prevent the heart from speaking unfavourably about the deceased.

The eyes of the god **Horus** were painted on the outside of coffins so that the mummy inside could see the world of the living. A tiny false door allowed the spirit to leave and re-enter the coffin.

In 1100 BC the Mayor of Thebes discovered that the royal tombs were being systematically **looted** – by the guards hired to protect them.

The Arabs produced a volume known as **The Book of Buried Pearls** specifically for tomb robbing, with detailed lists of hidden treasure and magic formulae for outwitting the guardian spirits.

Among the most amazing discoveries ever made in Egypt were two **burial caches** found at Thebes in the last century, containing no fewer than 40 royal mummies. They included great pharaohs such as Seti I and Ramesses II.

The mummy of **Ramesses I**, after its discovery at Thebes, was kept lying so long in the sun that the resins grew warm and the king's arm began to lift, terrifying the workmen nearby.

When some of the **Theban royal mummies** were shipped to the Cairo Museum they had a tax levied on them by the city authorities. There being no suitable tariff for 'mummy', eight of Egypt's greatest pharaohs were classed as 'dried fish'!

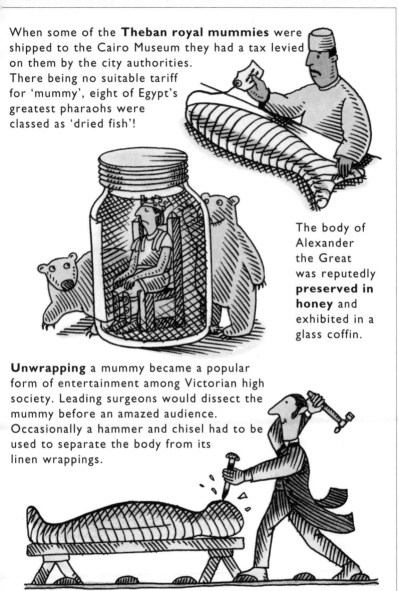

The body of Alexander the Great was reputedly **preserved in honey** and exhibited in a glass coffin.

Unwrapping a mummy became a popular form of entertainment among Victorian high society. Leading surgeons would dissect the mummy before an amazed audience. Occasionally a hammer and chisel had to be used to separate the body from its linen wrappings.

A bizarre 19th-century story records that a dealer at Thebes sold a recently **dead Italian** doctor to an English collector as a remarkably preserved ancient mummy. The 'mummy' was duly shipped to England.

The earliest **fingerprint** on record, from a mummy's hand in the British Museum, is filed in Scotland Yard's fingerprint department.

At the turn of the century about 300,000 **cat mummies** were shipped to Liverpool, to be converted into fertilizer.

Four million embalmed **ibises** were discovered at a single animal cemetery at Saqqara, each in its own individual pot.

The famous myth of the '**mummy's curse**' arose from the discovery of Tutankhamun's tomb in 1922. Five months after the tomb was revealed, its joint discoverer, Lord Carnarvon, died suddenly. The popular press attributed his demise to the pharaoh's anger at being disturbed – the 'Curse of Osiris'.

At the moment of **Lord Carnarvon**'s death, it was alleged, all the lights went out in Cairo. At the same time, in England, his faithful pet terrier howled and dropped dead.

In 1932 Boris Karloff starred in **The Mummy**, the first in a long line of Hollywood movies where a mummy-monster is brought back to life. Karloff's appearance in the film was based on the real mummy of Ramesses III.

In its 1971 Christmas catalogue, a Dallas department store offered 'His and Hers authenticated **mummy cases**, both approximately 2,000 years old – companions from the past, richly adorned but gratefully vacant.'

Ancient Egyptian history is conventionally divided into three main periods known as the Old Kingdom (c. 2613-2160 BC), Middle Kingdom (c. 2040-1750 BC) and New Kingdom (c. 1550-1086 BC). During these epochs the centralized power of the pharaohs was at its height, but between them came times of royal weakness, civil war and foreign invasion called Intermediate Periods. Later Egyptian history was characterized by further foreign invasions by the Libyans, Assyrians, Nubians, Persians and Greeks, whose kings often themselves became pharaohs. With the death of Cleopatra in 30 BC and the absorption of Egypt into the Roman Empire, the pharaonic era finally ended.

In the 3rd century BC an Egyptian priest called Manetho wrote a history of Egypt, dividing the list of kings into 30 dynasties or family lines. Scholars today use Manetho's subdivisions, sometimes adding a 31st dynasty at the end.

© 1994 Thames and Hudson Ltd
30 Bloomsbury Street, London WC1B 3QP

British Library Cataloguing-in-Publication Data

A catalogue record for this book is available from the British Library

ISBN 0-500-01629-1

Printed and bound in Slovenia by Mladinska Knjiga